With love and gratitude

To

From

Mother

new seasons™

a division of Publications International, Ltd.

Art Resource: Giraudon; Erich Lessing; © 1999 **Artists Rights Society (ARS), New York:** *Portrait of a Woman in a Fur Wrap* by Herman Richir/ADAGP, Paris; *Mother and Child* by Pablo Picasso/Estate of Pablo Picasso; **Bridgeman Art Library, London/New York:**
Mother and Child on a Green Background by Mary Cassatt, Reunion des Musees Nationaux; *Mother Combing Sara's Hair* by Mary Cassatt, Christie's Images, London; *Women Reading* by Mary Cassatt, Hirschl and Adler Galleries, New York; *Young Mother with Child Asleep in Her Lap* by William Lee-Hankey, Private Collection/Manya Igel Fine Arts Ltd., London; *Breakfast Time* by Norman Hepple, Bonhams, London; *Portrait of the artist's wife, Lady Pansy Pakenham, and Daughter* by Henry Lamb, Cheltenham Art Gallery & Museums, Gloucestershire, UK; *Girl Arranging Flowers* by William McGregor Paxton, Brooklyn Museum of Art, New York; *Sunrise, Brent at Low Water* by Julian Novorol, Private Collection/Bridgeman Art Library, London/New York; **Corbis; Planet Art; SuperStock;** Art Trade, Bonhams, London/Bridgeman Art Library, London/New York; Christie's Images; David David Gallery, Philadelphia; National Museum of American Art, Smithsonian Institution, Washington, D.C.

Original inspirations by:
Lain Chroust Ehmann
Marie Jones
Donna Shryer
Tricia Toney

Compiled inspirations by Joan Loshek

Copyright © 2000 Publications International, Ltd. All rights reserved. This book may not be reproduced or quoted in whole or in part by any means whatsoever without written permission from:

Louis Weber, CEO
Publications International, Ltd.
7373 North Cicero Avenue
Lincolnwood, Illinois 60712

Permission is never granted for commercial purposes.

Manufactured in China.

8 7 6 5 4 3 2 1

ISBN: 0-7853-3347-9

A mother, a rosebud,

early in the morning,

dew still on her petals,

begins her work,

unfurling as the sun shines higher,

with more beauty every minute,

making the thorns of life lovely,

freshening the summer air,

making this world a beautiful place.

Even when you're grown, adult and mature, in the eyes of a mother you are her child still.

A mother's instinct tells
her when to protect her young.
Her intuition tells her when
to let her young roam free.
I thank you, Mother, for always
knowing just when to hold me
close and when to let me fly.

A mother wears patience as a halo.

No length of time or distance

can weaken the bond between

mother and child.

There is no friendship, no love,

like that of the mother for the child.

Henry Ward Beecher

Photo

As an infant wraps his
hand around a mother's finger,
a circle of love is born.

$\mathscr{S}$ometimes the best thing I can do as a mother is to remember what it was like to be a child.

$\mathcal{O}$ur only job as mothers is to preserve the inquisitive, beautiful, knowing souls that are our children.

A giving mother is invaluable to a child.

A mother is the truest friend we have when trials, heavy and sudden,

fall upon us; when adversity takes the place of prosperity.

WASHINGTON IRVING

Sometimes it is right to share our wisdom and lead those we love to correct answers. Other times it is far wiser to stand quietly in the shadows, allowing someone dear to stumble upon her own answers.

Watch a child conquer his world.

Curiosity over a faraway object leads to walking.

The need to voice an opinion leads to speaking.

Allow yourself to be a child again,

discovering and accomplishing new things.

A mother is someone
who loves and
supports you as you
pursue your dreams.

*L*et me see myself through my child's eyes.

*L*et me listen as much as I speak.

*L*et me honor all in my child that makes him unique.

*L*et me be the kind of parent I know I can be.

Watch your child's face as she celebrates life.

Learn from your child.

Her lessons are illuminating.

The greatest gifts we can give our children are
unconditional love, open arms, and a willing ear.

The power within a mother's touch is nothing short of miraculous. With one sweep across a weary forehead, one turn of a wayward curl, merely mortal fingers can bring divine peace and blissful slumber.

There was never a
great man who had
not a great mother.
OLIVE SCHREINER

I am my mother's child.

Her vision created me.

Her dream manifested itself in me.

Her hope molded me.

Her love breathed life into me.

Her photo

I carry my mother's love with me always,
like a precious keepsake kept close to my heart.

Our children learn only what
we teach them. If we allow
ourselves to fly, to dream, to
love—they will do the same.

We never outgrow our need for our mother.
Her unconditional love provides an invisible
safety net as we walk along life's tightrope.

My life is a joyous reflection
of the love in my mother's heart,
the hope in my mother's soul,
and the strength in my mother's spirit.

Motherhood is defined not by grand gestures but by seemingly insignificant moments: a hug in the morning before the school bus comes, holding a child as he falls asleep, kissing the "owie" to make it all better. These are the things our children will remember.

Mothers are the center of
everything in a child's life: nourishment,
comfort, and always, love.

A mother's kindness is comfort food

for a hungry soul.

A mother's gentleness is soothing drink

for a thirsty heart.

She dries the tears from my sorrow.

She shares the joys of my achievements.

She listens to the source of my fears.

She encourages me to live fully in this world.

She is my friend. She is my teacher. She is my mother.

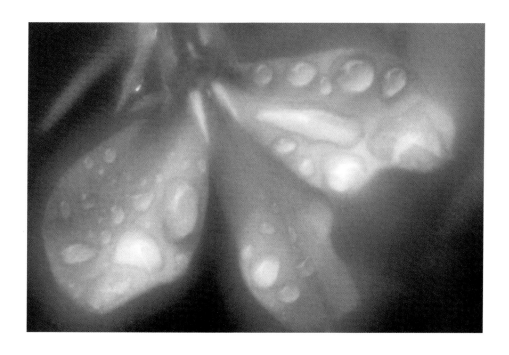

When I look in my child's eyes, I see the past—the many limbs of the family tree reaching forward to meet in this unique soul.

When I look in my child's eyes, I see the present—the ability to grab each moment and squeeze out each delicious drop.

When I look in my child's eyes, I see the future— all that she will be, all that she will do.

A Lullaby

Amazing Grace,
a mother's face,
a gentle, loving sight.

Arms wrapped like wings,
this angel sings,
a voice so clear and bright.

I rest my soul
basked in the glow
of her protective light.

Amazing Grace,
a peaceful place.
A lullaby goodnight.

Motherhood has no rules,
no report cards, no grades.
Its only guidelines are
these: Trust in yourself,
believe in your child, and
listen to your heart.

Mothers view their children
not through rose-colored glasses,
but through love-colored eyes.

Babies are gifts from
the angels; mothers
are gifts from God.

My mother's love is the gift of
wings that let my spirit take flight.

A mother gives birth not just to a child,
but to a greater vision of love and joy
than she could ever hope for herself.

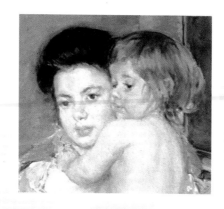

The way my mother loved me,

strong and kind and true,

has given me the confidence

to do all I can do.

The way my mother raised me,

joyful, bold, and free,

has given me the self-esteem

to be all I can be.

Our photo

I am my mother's child. You can see it in our smiles.

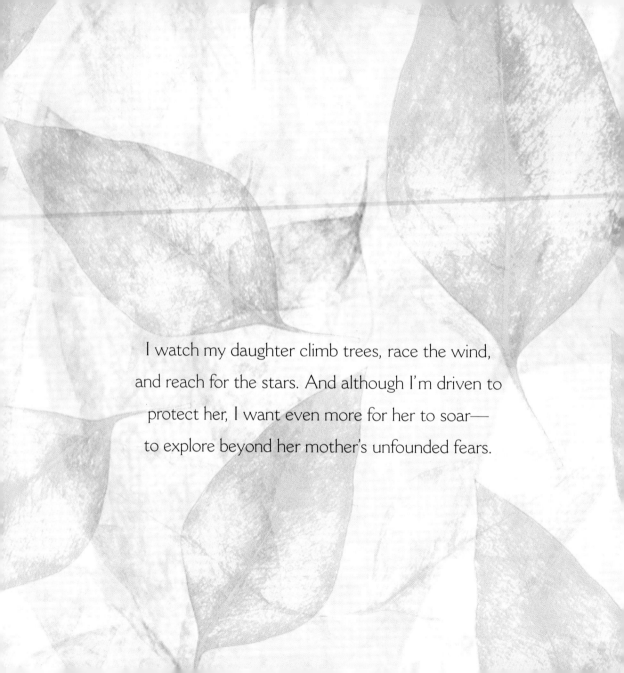

I watch my daughter climb trees, race the wind,
and reach for the stars. And although I'm driven to
protect her, I want even more for her to soar—
to explore beyond her mother's unfounded fears.

The path of motherhood can take unexpected turns.
But it is in its twists and turns, its hills and valleys,
that we experience new and surprising joys.

Mothers are given the greatest
treasure any human can know:
the knowledge that we do make a
difference in someone else's life.

Look into a mother's eyes
and here is what you'll see:
a vision of the happy soul
she hopes her child will be.

*A*t mother's knee,

listening to her read a story,

leaning against her as she kisses my head,

wondering at the pictures in the book she holds,

I feel comfortable and warm,

enveloped in her love.

Mother,

strong and sweet,

your gentle voice

brings joy.

Your love

never ceases.

A mother's unconditional love is

a safety net allowing her children

to take the necessary leaps of faith

to make their hopes and

dreams come true.

The greatest gift my mother gave to me was her
unwavering belief in my potential. I am all that I am today
because she never stopped believing in what I could be.

I cannot show my children perfection, but I can illustrate excellence.

I cannot always give them their way, but I can demonstrate compromise.

I cannot make their path easy, but I can help them learn determination.

I cannot keep them from feeling pain, but I can teach them how to love.

The best mothers are
those who know they
will not be perfect, that
they will make mistakes.
From this humility
springs mastery.

... What do girls do who haven't any mothers

to help them through their troubles?

LOUISA MAY ALCOTT

The dreams my mother dreamed for me

are now all coming true:

a happy home and family

and work I love to do.

As I look back upon my life

of one thing I am sure:

for every blessing I can count,

I owe it all to her.

Mothers not only raise children, we burnish souls and groom spirits. We are the guardians of the future.

Photo

There is no pride greater than that of a mother watching her children walk from her protection into lives of their own.

When I am plodding through my day,
thoroughly immersed in life's present drama,
my mother's love opens my eyes to pleasant
events, happy endings, and hidden treasures.

When I'm lonely and afraid
    you whisper, "Child, fear not."
When I simply can't go on
    you say, "Take one more shot."
When nothing seems to
    go my way you tell me,
    "Trust . . . you'll see!"
Like an angel on my shoulder,
    Mom, you're always
    there for me.

We spend so much time trying to soften our clothes, our hair, and our skin, that we often forget to soften our hearts. But our mothers know that a gentle heart is free, and its benefits are priceless.

You must sit down and rest your weary body

precisely when you have no time to do so.

When we continue beyond all hope, when we give even after we feel we have nothing left...it is only . then that we learn the true depths of our strength and love as mothers.

As rebellious teenagers,
we think becoming like our mothers is a curse.
As adults, we realize that becoming like our
mothers is nothing short of an honor.